First Phrases from Around the World

Everyday Spanish

Kim Thompson

Little Mitchie
an imprint of Mitchell Lane

Creating Young Nonfiction Readers

Little Mitchie lets children delve into nonfiction at beginning reading levels. Young readers are introduced to new concepts, facts, ideas, and vocabulary.

Tips for Reading Nonfiction with Young Readers

Talk about Nonfiction

Begin by explaining that nonfiction books give us information that is true. The book will be organized around a specific topic or idea, and we may learn new facts through reading.

Look at the Parts

Most nonfiction books have helpful features. Our *Little Mitchie* titles include color photographs and graphic aids, a table of contents, and an index. Share the purpose of these features with your reader.

Color Photos and Graphic Aids

A lot of information can be found by "reading" photos, charts, maps, and other graphic aids found within nonfiction texts. Help your reader learn more about the different ways information can be displayed.

Table of Contents

Located at the front of the book, this list shows the big ideas within the text and the page numbers where they can be found.

Index

Located at the back of the book, an index is an alphabetical list of topics and the page numbers where they can be found.

With a little help and guidance about reading nonfiction, you can feel good about introducing a young reader to the world of *Little Mitchie* nonfiction books.

Mitchell Lane
PUBLISHERS

2001 SW 31st Avenue
Hallandale, FL 33009
www.mitchelllanepub.com

Little Mitchie

First Edition, 2026.

Author: Kim Thompson
Designer: Kathy Walsh
Editor: Tricia Hoffman

Names/credits: Kim Thompson
Title: First Phrases from Around the World
Everyday Spanish
Description: Hallandale, FL:
Mitchell Lane Publishers, [2026]

Series: First Phrases from Around the World
Library bound ISBN: 979-8-89260-543-4
Paperback ISBN: 979-8-89260-585-4
eBook ISBN: 979-8-89260-546-5

Little Mitchie is an imprint of
Mitchell Lane Publishers

PHOTO CREDITS
Cover and Title pg: Adobe Stock: iukhym_vova, smile3377; Doodle Art Adobe: devitaayu, FourLeafLover, wanchana, veekicl, Rizky, mhatzapa, Kebon doodle, Asyam Design, piixypeach, syoko: p5, riza1999: istock: background, rica nohara; p7, Aneduard; p10, Hispanolistic, PeopleImages; p13, Bet_Noire, ktmoffitt; p14, Fernanda Reyes; p16, Tatsushi Takada; p17, curtoicurto; p20, martinedoucet, PeopleImages; p21, Hispanolistic, gerrantraite: Shutterstock: p4, TheVisualsYouNeed, ViDIStudio, Roman Samborskyi; p5 & 6, Roman Samborskyi; p6, stockpexel; p7, Eric Isselee; p9, Luis Molinero; p11, Wpadington; p12, Chiociolla, Chase D'animulls, BongoStock; p14, ESB Professional, Krakenimages.com; p15, Yuri A, Prostock-studio; p16, Roman Samborskyi, Alan Mazzocco; p17, sashahaltam; p18, Hananeko_Studio, spass; p19, Monkey Business Images, Sergey Novikov; p20, Kleber Cordeiro, Manny DaCunha; p22, fizkes, Kateholms, Africa Studio; p23, antoniodiaz

Table of Contents

This Is Me

Tengo ocho años.

I am eight years old.

Mi nombre es Valentina.

My name is Valentina.

Este soy yo

uno
one
dos
two
tres
three
cuatro
four
cinco
five
seis
six
siete
seven
ocho
eight
nueve
nine
diez
ten

¡Adiós!
Goodbye!

People and Pets

Vivo con mi familia.

I live with my family.

padre
father

madre
mother

hermano
brother

hermana
sister

Personas y mascotas

Tengo mascotas.

I have pets.

perro
dog

gato
cat

pájaro
bird

lagarto
lizard

ratón
mouse

conejo
rabbit

Today

Hoy es martes.
Today is Tuesday.

domingo
Sunday
lunes
Monday
martes
Tuesday
miércoles
Wednesday
jueves
Thursday
viernes
Friday
sábado
Saturday

El mes es octubre.
The month is October.

enero . . . . January
febrero . . . . . . February
marzo . . . . March
abril . . . . April
mayo . . . . May
junio. . . . . June
julio . . . . July
agosto . . . . August
septiembre . . . September
octubre . . . . October
noviembre . . . November
diciembre . . . . December

Hoy

soleado
sunny

frío
cold

lluvioso
rainy

ventoso
windy

Morning

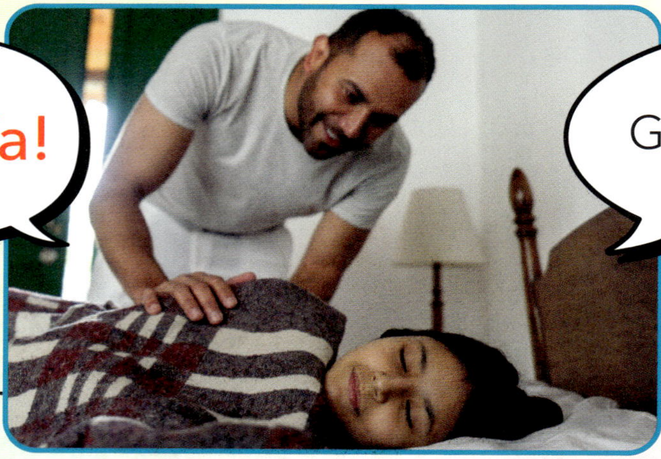

Me peino el cabello.

I comb my hair.

Me cepillo los dientes.

I brush my teeth.

Mañana

Yo llevo una camisa roja.

I wear a red shirt.

naranja orange	amarillo yellow		azul blue	verde green
púrpura purple	rojo red	rosa pink	negro black	blanco white

Breakfast

Quiero cereal para el desayuno, por favor.

I want cereal for breakfast, please.

tostada
toast

jugo de naranja
orange juice

tocino
bacon

huevo
egg

Desayuno

El autobús ya está aquí. ¡Es hora de partir!

The bus is here. It is time to go!

autobús escolar
school bus

mochila
backpack

School

Voy a la escuela.

I go to school.

Yo leo.

I read.

Yo hago matemáticas.

I do math.

Escuela

Necesito ayuda.
I need help.

maestra
teacher

escritorio
desk

¿Puedo ir al baño?
May I go to the bathroom?

Time to Play

¿Jugarás conmigo?

Will you play with me?

¡Sí!

Yes!

Yo corro.
I run.

Yo me balanceo.
I swing.

Hora de jugar

Lanzo una pelota.

I throw a ball.

Neighborhood

Yo vivo en un barrio.

I live in a neighborhood.

Saludo a mi amigo.

I wave to my friend.

Voy a la tienda.

I go to the store.

Vecindario

¿Cuanto cuesta esto?

How much does this cost?

árbol
tree

flores
flowers

acera
sidewalk

edificio
building

agua
water

bicicleta
bicycle

Dinner

Sí, por favor.
Yes, please.

No, gracias.
No, thank you.

Disculpe.
Excuse me.

Cena

Me gusta la comida mexicana.

I like Mexican food.

nachos
nachos

quesadilla
quesadilla

tacos
tacos

burrito
burrito

Me gusta la comida americana.

I like American food.

hamburguesa
hamburger

papas fritas
french fries

Night

Yo uso pijama.

I wear pajamas.

Me voy a la cama.

I go to bed.

Cierro los ojos.

I close my eyes.

Noche

oso de peluche
teddy bear

Index

About Spanish

Spanish is the first language of more than 400 million people. It is the fourth most common language in the world. The top five countries where Spanish is spoken are Mexico, Colombia, Argentina, the United States, and Spain. Spanish is the official language in 18 countries in Latin America and South America. It is also the official language of Spain on the continent of Europe and Equatorial Guinea on the continent of Africa.